ANIMALS

INFO PICS

BY HARRIET BRUNDLE

BookLife
PUBLISHING

©2019
BookLife Publishing Ltd.
King's Lynn
Norfolk PE30 4LS

All rights reserved.
Printed in Malaysia.

A catalogue record for this
book is available from the
British Library.

ISBN: 978-1-78637-914-6

Written by:
Harriet Brundle

Edited by:
Emilie Dufresne

Designed by:
Danielle Rippengill

Image Credits

Cover and throughout – Bukhavets Mikhail, Maquiladora, Tarikdiz, Platonova Sveta, Elena Paletskaya, Taras Dubov, Babich A Aleksey, Bhonard. 4&5 – Nadya_Art. 6&7 – tinkivinki, Nitchy333, Inspiring, Alx.Suvorov. 8&9 – VectorShow, ArnyGFX. 10&11 – MSSA, Roi and Roi, NotionPic, MarySan. 12&13 – YUCALORA, 792442699. 14&15 – Margaret Jone Wollman, Mr. Luck, Oceloti. 16&17 – Lana_Samcorp, CloudyStock. 18&19 – MuchMania, graphixmania, romawka, lukpedclub. 20&21 – Nadya_Art, puruan, Nadzin. All images courtesy of Shutterstock.com. With thanks to Getty Images, Thinkstock Photo and iStockphoto.

CONTENTS

Words that look like <u>this</u> can be found in the glossary on page 24.

MAMMALS

All mammals have backbones. Any animal that has a backbone is called a vertebrate.

Female mammals make milk in their <u>mammary glands</u> so that they can feed their <u>young</u>.

4

Mammals are <u>warm-blooded</u> animals.

Most mammals have hair or fur on their bodies. Even dolphins have some hair on their bodies.

Most mammals give birth to live young.

5

Bats are the only mammals that can fly.

Mammals live in different <u>habitats</u> all around the world. Mammals can live on land or even under water.

Humans are mammals.

Mammals use lungs to breathe.

The blue whale and the African elephant are two of the biggest mammals on Earth.

Mammals that live in water, such as seals, come to the <u>surface</u> for the air they need.

REPTILES

Reptiles can be covered in scales, have a hard shell, or even have both. Lizards and turtles are types of reptiles.

Reptiles are also vertebrates.

Reptiles are cold-blooded animals.

This means that reptiles need to move into either the sunshine or the shade to keep themselves at the right temperature.

It is thought that reptiles have lived on Earth for millions of years.

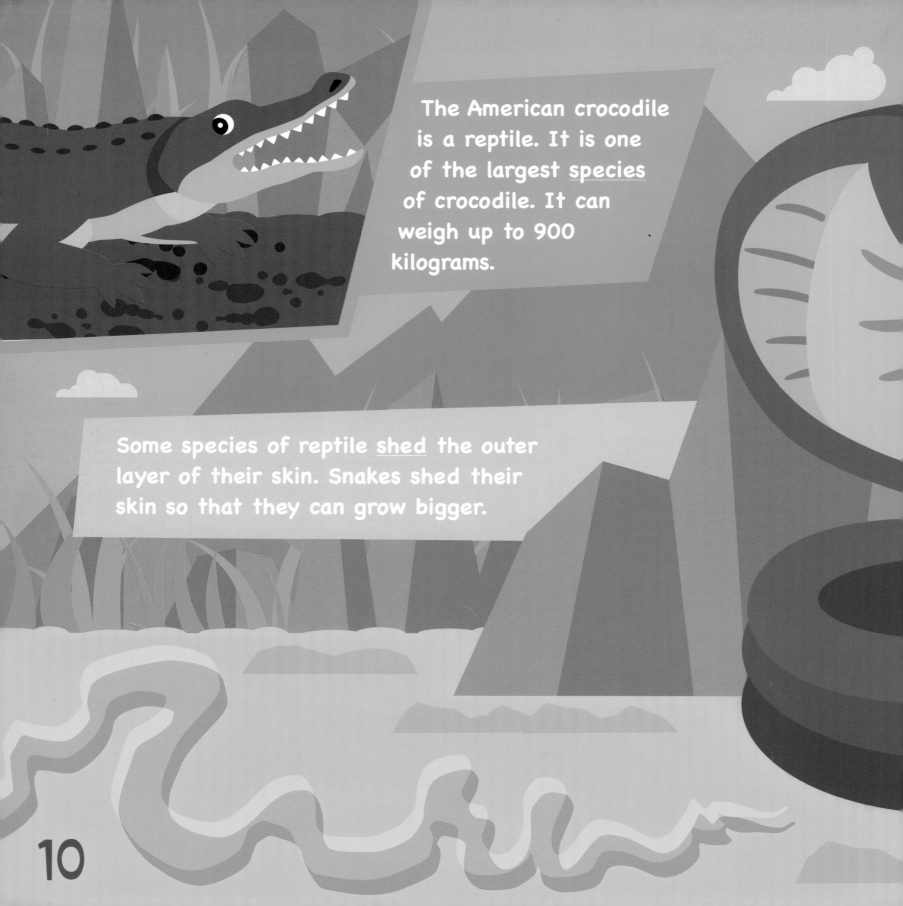

The American crocodile is a reptile. It is one of the largest <u>species</u> of crocodile. It can weigh up to 900 kilograms.

Some species of reptile <u>shed</u> the outer layer of their skin. Snakes shed their skin so that they can grow bigger.

10

Most reptiles lay eggs.
A few species of reptile
give birth to live young.

Reptiles can live on land or in water.

AMPHIBIANS

Amphibians are cold-blooded animals.

Amphibians are vertebrates.
They usually live in damp areas,
such as ponds or rainforests.

Most amphibians have thin skin
that they use to help them breathe.

Frogs don't chew their food;
they swallow it whole.

12

Frogs are a type of amphibian that eat insects such as flies and dragonflies.

Amphibians can usually live on land and in water.

Frogs, toads and salamanders are all amphibians.

13

The Chinese giant salamander is one of the largest amphibians on Earth.

Amphibians need their habitat to stay the same. Any changes to their habitat can cause them harm.

14

BIRDS

Birds have hard beaks and no teeth.

Birds have feathers. Their feathers help to keep them warm and can be used to attract other birds or for camouflage.

Birds are warm-blooded vertebrates.

Birds can feed their chicks things such as worms, insects and berries.

Birds lay eggs that have hard shells. The eggs usually need to be kept warm before the chicks are ready to hatch.

17

There are thousands of different species of bird.

Lots of birds <u>migrate</u> every year.

A bird might have to fly a very long way during migration. Birds migrate for many reasons, such as searching for warmer areas, looking for food and finding somewhere to lay their eggs.

All birds have wings but not all can fly. Penguins are a type of bird that cannot fly.

Ostriches lay the largest eggs of any bird.

One ostrich egg was recorded as weighing over two and a half kilograms.

19

FISH

Fish are vertebrates.

Fish have gills that they use to breathe under water.

Their gills often look like small slits on the sides of their body.

Almost all fish are cold-blooded.

Sailfish and the black marlin fish are two of the fastest species of fish in the ocean.

Sharks are a type of fish.

The great white shark can grow to around six metres in length.

INVERTEBRATES

Some species of animals do not have a backbone. These animals are known as invertebrates.

Animals such as worms, jellyfish, insects and spiders are all invertebrates.

Some invertebrates, such as worms, have very soft bodies. Others, such as beetles, have a hard outer shell. This shell is called an exoskeleton.

Over nine-tenths of all animals in the world are invertebrates.

Spiders are invertebrates. One of the largest spiders on Earth is the Goliath bird-eating tarantula.

GLOSSARY

attract	to get the attention of
camouflage	traits that allow an animal to hide itself in a habitat
cold-blooded	animals that have blood that changes with the temperature around them
habitats	the natural homes in which animals or plants live
mammary glands	the parts of the body that make milk
migrate	to move from one place to another based on changing needs
shed	to lose old skin or hair, in order to make way for new skin or hair growing underneath
species	a group of very similar animals or plants that can create young together
surface	the outer part or top of something
temperature	how hot or cold something is
warm-blooded	animals that have blood that stays at a steady and warm temperature
young	an animal's offspring or babies

INDEX